Tvrba

Philosophorvm

OR

ASSEMBLY OF THE SAGES

CALLED ALSO

THE BOOK OF TRUTH IN THE ART

AND THE THIRD PYTHAGORICAL SYNOD

ANCIENT ALCHEMICAL TREATISE TRANSLATED FROM
THE LATIN, THE CHIEF READINGS OF THE SHORTER
CODEX, PARALLELS FROM THE GREEK ALCHEMISTS,
AND EXPLANATIONS OF OBSCURE TERMS

BY

ARTHUR EDWARD WAITE

PREFACE.

Turba Philosophorum is indisputably the most ancient extant treatise on Alchemy in the Latin tongue, but it was not, so far as can be ascertained, originally written in Latin ; the compiler or editor, for in many respects it can scarcely be regarded as an original composition, wrote either in Hebrew or Arabic ; however, the work, not only at the present day, but seemingly during the six or seven centuries when it was quoted as an authority by all the alchemical adepts, has been familiar only in its Latin garb. It is not, of course, certain that the original is irretrievably lost, the Arabic and Syriac manuscripts treating of early chemistry are preserved in considerable numbers in the various libraries of Europe, and have only been imperfectly explored. Unfortunately, the present editor has neither the opportunity nor the qualifications for undertaking such a task.

There are two codices or recensions of The Turba Philosophorum, which differ considerably from one another. What is called in the following pages the second recension, is appreciably shorter, clearer, and, on the whole, the less corrupt of the two, but they are both in a bad state. The longer recension has been chosen for the text of the following translation, because it seemed desirable to give the work in its entirety. The variations of the second recension are appended usually in foot-notes, but where the reading of the text is so corrupt as to be quite untranslatable, the editor has occasionally substituted that of the alternative version, and has in most cases indicated the course pursued.

Monsieur Berthelot's invaluable text and translation of the Byzantine Alchemists has been largely made use of, to illustrate the striking analogies between the Greek Hermetic writers of the fourth century and the Turba. It is to this great scholar and scientist that we owe the discovery of these analogies, some of which are very clearly indicated in a chapter devoted to the subject, and forming part of his " Essai sur la Transmission de la Science Antique au Moyen Age." It follows from M. Berthelot's researches, that Latin Alchemy, which has always been rightly referred to an Arabian source, connects with the Greek Alchemy which preceded Arabian Science, because the latter was itself derived from Greece. We are also enabled to identify, for the first time, and that with perfect certainty, those ancient sages, to whom all the Latin literature makes requent and reverent allusion ; we now know that they are Zosimus, the Panopolite, the adepts of the school of Democritus, and the other writers preserved in the Byzantine collection. M. Berthelot, however, infers that the Greek influence found in The Turba Philosophorum was not a direct influence, but was derived mediately through channels which are now unknown In any case the Turba summarises the author's preceding Geber, and is therefore the most valuable, as it is the most ancient, treatise on Alchemy, which exists in the Latin language.

The chief printed versions of The Turba Philosophorum, are those of the " Theatrum Chemicum," the "BibKotheca Chemica Curiosa," and that of the smaller collection entitled " Artis Auriferae Tractatus." There are some translations of the work existing in German and some also in French. Those in the latter language are specially remarkable for the very slender way in which they represent the original. The versions contained in Salmon's " Bibliotheque des Philosophes Alchimiques," and in the " Tro'S Anciens Traictes de la Philosophic Naturelle," are instances in point. One English version in manuscript is known to the present editor, and it will be found in the British Museum amongst the treasures of the Sloane collection. It is rendered, however, from the French, and has been found useless for the purposes of this translation.

It may be added that the great collections of Alchemy, such as he " Theatrum Chemicum " and Mangetus, contain colloquies, ommentaries, and enigmas which pretend to elucidate the ysteries of The Turba Philosophorum. While they are of a onsiderably later date, they at the same time belong to the early period of Latin Alchemy. It may be added also that the editor has collected a considerable amount of material concerning this curious work, which the limits of the present volume preclude him from utilising.

ARTHUR EDWARD WAITE.

THE TURBA PHILOSOPHORUM,

TAKEN FROM AN ANCIENT MANUSCRIPT CODEX,

MORE PERFECT THAN ANY EDITION

PUBLISHED HERETOFORE.

The Turba Philosophorum.

The Epistle of Arisleus, prefixed to the Words of the Sages, concerning the Purport of this Book, for the Benefit of Posterity, and the same being as here follows:-

Arisleus, begotten of Pythagoras, a disciple of the disciples by the grace of thrice great Hermes, learning from the seat of knowledge, unto all who come after wisheth health and mercy. I testify that my master, Pythagoras, the Italian, master of the wise and chief of the Prophets, had a greater gift of God and of Wisdom than was granted to any one after Hermes. Therefore he had a mind to assemble his disciples, who were now greatly increased, and had been constituted the chief persons throughout all regions for the discussion of this most precious Art, that their words might be a foundation for posterity. He then commanded Iximidrus, of highest council, to be the first speaker, who said:-

The First Dictum.

Iximidrus Saith:- I testify that the beginning of all things is a Certain Nature, which is perpetual, coequalling all things, and that the visible natures, with their births and decay, are times wherein the ends to which that nature brings them are beheld and summoned. Now, I instruct you that the stars are igneous, and are kept within bounds by the air. If the humidity and density of the air did not exist to separate the flames of the sun from living things, then the Sun would consume all creatures. But God has provided the separating air, lest that which He has created should be burnt up. Do you not: observe that the Sun when it rises in the heaven overcomes the air by its heat, and that the warmth penetrates from the upper to the lower parts of the air? If, then, the air did not presently breathe forth those winds whereby creatures are generated, the Sun by its heat would certainly destroy all that lives. But the Sun is kept in check by the air, which thus conquers because it unites the heat of the Sun to its own heat, and the humidity of water to its own humidity. Have you not remarked how tenuous water is drawn up into the air by the action of the heat of the Sun, which thus helps the water against itself? If the water did not nourish the air by such tenuous moisture, assuredly the Sun would overcome the air. The fire, therefore, extracts moisture from the water, by means of which the air conquers the fire itself. Thus, fire and water are enemies between which there is no consanguinity, for the fire is hot and dry, but the water is cold and moist. The air, which is warm and moist, joins these together by its concording medium; between the humidity of water and the heat of fire the air is thus placed to establish peace. rind look ye all how there shall arise a spirit from the tenuous vapour of the air, because the heat being joined to the humour, there necessarily issues something tenuous, which will become a wind. For the heat of the Sun extracts something tenuous out of the air, which also becomes spirit and life to all creatures. All this, however, is disposed in such manner by the will of God, and a coruscation appears when the heat of the Sun touches and breaks up a cloud.

The Turba saith:- Well hast thou described the fire, even as thou knowest concerning it, and thou hast believed the word of thy brother.

The Second Dictum.

Exumedrus saith:- I do magnify the air according to the mighty speech of Iximidrus, for the work is improved thereby. The air is inspissated, and it is also made thin; it grows warm and becomes cold. The inspissation thereof takes place when it is divided in heaven by the elongation of the Sun; its rarefaction is when, by the exaltation of the Sun in heaven, the air becomes warm and is rarefied. It is comparable with the complexion of Spring, in the distinction of time, which is neither warm nor cold. For according to the mutation of the constituted disposition with the altering distinctions of the soul, so is Winter altered. The air, therefore, is inspissated when the Sun is removed from it, and then cold supervenes upon men.

Whereat the Turba said:- Excellently hast thou described the air, and given account of what thou knowest to be therein.

The Third Dictum.

Anaxagoras saith:- I make known that the beginning of all those things which God hath created is weight and proportion, for weight rules all things, and the weight and spissitude of the earth is manifest in proportion; but weight is not found except in body. And know, all ye Turba, that the spissitude of the four elements reposes in the earth; for the spissitude of fire falls into air, the spissitude of air, together with the spissitude received from the fire, falls into water; the spissitude also of water, increased by the spissitude of fire and air, reposes in earth. Have you not observed how the spissitude of the four elements is conjoined in earth! The same, therefore, is more inspissated than all.

Then saith the Turba:- Thou hast well spoken. Verily the earth is more inspissated than are the rest. Which, therefore, is the most rare of the four elements and is most worthy to possess the rarity of these four?

He answereth:- Fire is the most rare among all, and thereunto cometh what is rare of these four. But air is less rare than fire, because it is warm and moist, while fire is warm and dry; now that which is warm and dry is more rare than the warm and moist.

They say unto him:- The which element is of less rarity than air!

He answereth:- Water, since cold and moisture inhere therein, and every cold humid is of less rarity than a warm humid.

Then do they say unto him:- Thou hast spoken truly. What, therefore, is of less rarity than water?

He answereth:- Earth, because it is cold and dry, and that which is cold and dry is of less rarity than that which is cold and moist.

Pythagoras saith:- Well have ye provided, O Sons of the Doctrine, the description of these four natures, out of which God hath created all things. Blessed, therefore, is he who comprehends what ye have declared, for from the apex of the world he shall not find an intention greater than his own! Let us, therefore, make perfect our discourse.

They reply:- Direct every one to take up our speech in turn. Speak thou, O Pandolfus!

The Fourth Dictum.

But Pandolfus saith:- I signify to posterity that air is a tenuous matter of water, and that it is not: separated from it. It remains above the dry earth, to wit, the air hidden in the water, which is under the earth. If this air did not exist, the earth would not remain above the humid water.

They answer:- Thou hast said well; complete, therefore, thy speech.

But he continueth:- The air which is hidden in the water under the earth is that which sustains the earth, lest it should be plunged into the said water; and it, moreover, prevents the earth from being overflowed by that water. The province of the air is, therefore, to fill up and to make separation between diverse things, that is to say, water and earth, and it is constituted a peacemaker between hostile things, namely, water and fire, dividing these, lest they destroy one another.

The Turba saith:- If you gave an illustration hereof, it would be clearer to those who do not understand.

He answereth:- An egg is an illustration, for therein four things are conjoined; the visible cortex or shell represents the earth, and the albumen, for white part, is the water. But a very thin inner cortex is joined to the outer cortex, representing, as I have signified to you, the separating medium between earth and water, namely, that air which divides the earth from the water. The yolk also of the egg represents fire; the cortex which contains the yolk corresponds to that other air which separates the water from the fire. But they are both one and the same air, namely, that which separates things frigid, the earth from the water, and that which separates the water from the fire. But the lower air is thicker than the upper air, and the upper air is more rare and subtle, being nearer to the fire than the lower air. In the egg, therefore, are four things- earth, water, air, and fire. But the point of the Sun, these four excepted, is in the centre of the yolk, and this is the chicken. Consequently, all philosophers in this most excellent art have described the egg as an example, which same thing they have set over their work.

The Fifth Dictum.

Arisleus saith:- Know that the earth is a hill and not a plain, for which reason the Sun does not ascend over all the zones of the earth in a single hour; but if it were flat, the sun would rise in a moment over the whole earth.

Parmenides saith:- Thou hast spoken briefly, O Arisleus!

He answereth: Is there anything the Master has left us which bears witness otherwise? Yet I testify that God is one, having never engendered or been begotten, and that the head of all things after Him is earth and fire, because fire is tenuous and light, and it rules all things on earth, but the earth, being ponderous and gross, sustains all things which are ruled by fire.

The Sixth Dictum.

Lucas saith:- You speak only about four natures; and each one of you observes something concerning these. Now, I testify unto you that all things which God hath created are from these four natures, and the things which have been created out of them return into them, In these living creatures are generated and die, and all things take place as God hath predestinated.

Democritus, the disciple of Lucas, answereth:- Thou hast well spoken, O Lucas, when dealing with the four natures!

Then saith Arisleus:- O Democritus, since thy knowledge was derived from Lucas, it is presumption to speak among those who are well acquainted with thy master!

Lucas answereth:- albeit Democritus received from me the science of natural things, that knowledge was derived from the philosophers of the Indies and from the Babylonians; I think he surpasses those of his own age in this learning.

The Turba answereth:- When he attains to that age he will give no small satisfaction, but being in his youth he should keep silence.

The Seventh Dictum.

Lucusta saith:- All those creatures which have been described by Lucas are two only, of which one is neither known nor expressed, except by piety, for it is not seen or felt.

Pythagoras saith:- Thou hast entered upon a subject which, if completed, thou wilt describe subtly. State, therefore, what is this thing which is neither felt, seen, nor known.

Then he:- It is that which is not known, because in this world it is discerned by reason without the clients thereof, which are sight, hearing, taste, smell, and touch. O Crowd of the Philosophers, know you not that it Is only sight which can distinguish white from black, and hearing only which can discriminate between a good and bad word! Similarly, a wholesome odour cannot be separated by reason from one which is fetid, except through the sense of smell, nor can sweetness be discriminated from bitterness save by means of taste, nor smooth from rough unless by touch.

The Turba answereth:- Thou hast well spoken, yet hast thou omitted to treat of that particular thing which is not known, or described, except by reason and piety.

Saith he:- Are ye then in such haste! Know that the creature which is cognised in none of these five ways is a sublime creature, and, as such, is neither seen nor felt, but is perceived by reason alone, of which reason Nature confesses that God is a partaker.

They answer:- Thou hast spoken truly and excellently.

And he:- I will now give a further explanation. Know that this creature, that is to say, the world, hath a light, which is the Sun, and the same is more subtle than all other natures, which light is so ordered that living beings may attain to vision. But if this subtle light were removed, they would become darkened, seeing nothing, except the light of the moon, or of the stars, or of fire, all which are derived from the light of the Sun, which causes all creatures to give light. For this God has appointed the Sun to be the light of the world, by reason of the attenuated nature of the Sun. And know that the sublime creature before mentioned has no need of the light of this Sun, because the Sun is beneath that creature, which is more subtle and more lucid. This light, which is more lucid than the light of the Sun, they have taken from the light of God, which is more subtle than their light. Know also that the created world is composed of two dense things and two rare things, but nothing of the dense is in the sublime creature. Consequently the Sun is rarer than all inferior creatures.

The Turba answereth:- Thou hast excellently described what thou hast related. And if, good Master, thou shalt utter anything whereby our hearts may be vivified, which now are mortified by folly, thou wilt confer upon us a great boon!

The Eighth Dictum.

Pythagoras saith:- I affirm that God existed before all things, and with Him was nothing, as He was at first. But know, all ye Philosophers, that I declare this in order that I may fortify your opinion concerning these four elements and arcana, as well as in the sciences thereof, at which no one can arrive save by the will of God. Understand, that when God was alone, He created four things- fire, air, water, and earth, out of which things He afterwards created all others, both the sublime and the inferior, because He predestinated from the beginning that all creatures extracted from water should multiply and increase, that they might dwell in the world and perform His judgments therein. Consequently, before all, He created the four elements, out of which He afterwards created what He willed, that is to say, diverse creatures, some of which were produced from a single element.

The Turba saith:- Which are these, O Master!

And he:- They are the angels, whom He created out of fire.

But the Turba:- Which, then, are created out of two?

And he:- Out of the elements of fire and air are the sun, moon, and stars composed. Hence the angels are more lucid than the sun, moon, and stars, because they are created from one substance, which is less dense than two, while the sun and the stars are created from a composition of fire and air.

The Turba saith:- And what concerning the creation of Heaven?

Then he:- God created the Heaven out of water and air, whence this is also composed of two, namely, the second of the rarer things, which is air, and the second of the denser things, which is water.

And they:- Master, continue thy discourse concerning these three, and rejoice our hearts with thy sayings, which are life to the dead.

But the other answereth:- I notify to you that God hath further made creatures out of three and out of four; out of three are created flying things, beasts, and vegetables; some of these are created out of water, air, and earth, some out of fire, air, and earth.

But the Turba saith:- Distinguish these divers creatures one from another.

And he:- Beasts are created out of fire, air, and earth; dying things out of fire, air, and water, because flying things, and all among vegetables which have a spirit, are created out of water, while all brute animals are from earth, air, and fire. Yet in vegetables there is no fire, for they are created out of earth, water, and air.

Whereat the Turba saith:- Let us assume that a fire, with your reverence's pardon, does reside in vegetables.

And he:- Ye have spoken the truth, and I affirm that they contain fire.

And they:- Whence is that fire?

He answereth:- Out of the heat of the air which is concealed therein; for I have signified that a thin fire is present in the air, but the elementary fire concerning which you were in doubt is not produced, except in things which have spirit and soul. But out of four elements our father Adam and his sons were created, that is, of fire, air, water, and likewise earth. Understand, all ye that are wise, how everything which God hath created out of one essence dies not until the Day of Judgment. The definition of death is the disjunction of the composite, but there is no disjunction of that which is simple, for it is one. Death consists in the separation of the soul from the body, because anything formed out of two, three, or four components must disintegrate, and this is death. Understand, further, that no complex substance which lacks fire eats, drinks, or sleeps, because in all things which have a spirit fire is that which eats.

The Turba answereth:- How is it, Master, that the angels, being created of fire, do not eat, seeing thou assertest that fire is that which eats!

And he: Hence ye doubt, each having his opinion, and ye are become opponents, but if ye truly knew the elements, ye would not deny these things. I agree with all whose judgment it is that simple fire eats not, but thick fire. The angels, therefore, are not created out of thick fire, but out of the thinnest of very thin fire; being created, then, of that which is most simple and exceedingly thin, they neither eat, drink, nor sleep.

And the Turba:- Master, our faculties are able to perceive, for by God's assistance we have exhausted thy sayings, but our faculties of hearing and of sight are unable to carry such great things. May God reward thee for the sake of thy disciples, since it is with the object of instructing future generations that thou hast summoned us together from our countries, the recompense of which thou wilt not fail to receive from the Judge to come.

Arisleus saith:- Seeing that thou hast gathered us together for the advantage of posterity, I think that no explanations will be more useful than definitions of those four elements which thou hast taught us to attain.

And he:- None of you are, I suppose, ignorant that all the Wise have propounded definitions in God.

The Turba answereth:- Should your disciples pass over anything, it becomes you, O Master, to avoid omissions for the sake of future generations.

And he:- If it please you, I will begin the disposition here, since envious men in their books have separated that, or otherwise I will put it at the end of the book.

Whereat the Turba saith:- Place it where you think it will be dearest for future generations.

And he:- I will place it where it will not be recognised by the foolish, nor ignored by the Sons of the Doctrine, for it is the key, the perfection and the end.

The Ninth Dictum.

Eximenus saith:- God hath created all things by his word, having said unto them: Be, and they were made, with the four other elements, earth, water, air, and tire, which He coagulated, and things contrary were commingled, for we see that fire is hostile to water, water hostile to fire, and both are hostile to earth and air. Yet God hath united them peacefully, so that they love one another. Out of these four elements, therefore, are all things created- heaven and the throne thereof; the angels; the sun, moon. and stars; earth and sea, with all things that are in the sea, which indeed are various, and not alike, for their natures have been made diverse by God, and also the creations. But the diversity is more than I have stated; each of these natures is of diverse nature, and by a legion of diversities is the nature of each diverse. Now this diversity subsists in all creatures, because they were created out of diverse elements. Had they been created out of one element, they would have been agreeing natures. But diverse elements being here mingled, they lose their own natures, because the dry being mixed with the humid and the cold combined with the hot, become neither cold nor hot; so also the humid being mixed with the dry becomes neither dry nor humid. But when the four elements are commingled, they agree, and thence proceed creatures which never attain to perfection, except they be left by night to putrefy and become visibly corrupt. God further completed his creation by means of increase, food, life, and government. Sons of the Doctrine, not without purpose have I described to you the disposition of these four elements, for in them is a secret arcanum; two of them are perceptible to the sense of touch and vision, and of these the operation and virtue are well known. These are earth and water. But there are two other elements which are neither visible nor tangible, which yield naught, whereof the place is never seen, nor are their operations and force known, save in the former elements, namely, earth and water; now when the four elements are not commingled, no desire of men is accomplished. But being mixed, departing from their own natures, they become another thing. Over these let us meditate very carefully.

And the Turba:- Master, if you speak, we will give heed to Your words.

Then he:- I have now discoursed, and that well. I will speak only useful words which ye will follow as spoken. Know, all present, that no true tincture is made except from our copper. Do not therefore, exhaust your brains and your money, lest ye fill your hearts with sorrow. I will give you a fundamental axiom, that unless you turn the aforesaid copper into white, and make visible coins and then afterwards again turn it into redness, until a Tincture: results, verily, ye accomplish nothing. Burn therefore the copper, break it up, deprive it of its blackness by cooking, imbuing, and washing, until the same becomes white. Then rule it.

The Tenth Dictum.

Arisleus saith:- Know that the key of this work is the art of Coins. Take, therefore, the body which I have shewn to you and reduce it to thin tablets. Next immerse the said tablets in the Water of our Sea, which is permanent Water, and, after it is covered, set it over a gentle fire until the tablets are melted and become waters or Etheliae, which are one and the same thing. Mix, cook, and simmer in a gentle fire until Brodium is produced, like to Saginatum. Then stir in its water of Etheliae until it be coagulated, and the coins become variegated, which we call the Flower of Salt. Cook it, therefore, until it be deprived of blackness, and the whiteness appear. Then rub it, mix with the Gum of Gold, and cook until it becomes red Etheliae. Use patience in pounding lest you become weary. Imbue the Ethelia with its own water, which has preceded from it, which also is Permanent Water, until the same becomes red. This, then, is Burnt Copper, which is the Leaven of Gold and the Flower thereof. Cook the same with Permanent Water, which is always with it, until the water be dried up. Continue the operation until all the water is consumed, and it becomes a most subtle powder.

The Eleventh Dictum.

Parmenides saith:- Ye must know that envious men have dealt voluminously with several waters, brodiums, stones, and metals, seeking to deceive all you who aspire after knowledge. Leave, therefore, all these, and make the white red, out of this our copper, taking copper and lead, letting these stand for the grease, or blackness, and tin for the liquefaction. Know ye, further, that unless ye rule the Nature of Truth, and harmonize well together its complexions and compositions, the consanguineous with the consanguineous, and the first with the first, ye act improperly and effect nothing, because natures will meet their natures, follow them, and rejoice. For in them they putrefy and are generated, because Nature is ruled by Nature, which destroys it, turns it into dust, reduces to nothing, and finally herself renews it, repeats, and frequently produces the same. Therefore look in books, that ye may know the Nature of Truth, what putrefies it and what renews, what savour it possesses, what neighbours it naturally has, and how they love each other, how also after love enmity and corruption intervene, and how these natures should be united one to another and made at peace, until they become gentle in the fire in similar fashion. Having, therefore, noticed the facts in this Art, set your hands to the work. If indeed, ye know not the Natures of Truth, do not approach the work, since there will follow nothing but harm, disaster, and sadness. Consider, therefore, the teaching of the Wise, how they have declared the whole work in this saying:- Nature rejoices in Nature, and Nature contains Nature. In these words there is shewn forth unto you the whole work. Leave, therefore, manifold and superfluous things, and take quicksilver, coagulate in the body of Magnesia, in Kuhul, or in Sulphur which does not burn; make the same nature white, and place it upon our Copper, when it becomes white. And if ye cook still more, it becomes red, when if ye proceed to coction, it becomes gold. I tell you that it turns the sea itself into red and the colour of gold. Know ye also that gold is not turned into redness save by Permanent Water, because Nature rejoices in Nature.: Reduce, therefore, the same by means of cooking into a humour, until the hidden nature appear. If, therefore, it be manifested externally, seven times imbue the same with water, cooking, imbuing, and washing, until it become red. O those celestial natures, multiplying the natures of truth by the will of God! O that potent Nature, which overcame and conquered natures, and caused its natures to rejoice and be glad! This, therefore, is that special and spiritual nature to which the God thereof can give what fire cannot. Consequently, we glorify and magnify that [species], than which nothing is more precious in the true tincture, or the like in the smallest degree to be found. This is that truth which those investigating wisdom love. For when it is liquefied with bodies, the highest operation is effected. If ye knew the truth, what great thanks ye would give me! Learn, therefore, that while you are tingeing the cinders, you must destroy those that are mixed. For it overcomes those which are mixed, and changes them to its own colour. And as it visibly overcame the surface, even so it mastered the interior. And if one be volatile but the other endure the fire, either joined to the other endures the fire. Know also, that if the vapours have whitened the surfaces, they will certainly whiten the interiors. Know further, all ye seekers after Wisdom, that one matter overcomes four, and our Sulphur alone consumes all things.

The Turba answereth: Thou hast spoken excellently well, O Parmenides, but thou hast not demonstrated the disposition of the smoke to posterity, nor how the same is whitened!

The Twelfth Dictum.

Lucas saith: I will speak at this time, following the steps of the ancients. Know, therefore, all ye seekers after Wisdom, that this treatise is not from the beginning of the ruling! Take quicksilver, which is from the male, and coagulate according to custom. Observe that I am speaking to you in accordance with custom, because it has been already coagulated. Here, therefore, is not the beginning of the ruling, but I prescribe this method, namely, that you shall take the quicksilver from the male, and shall either impose upon iron, tin, or governed copper, and it will be whitened. White Magnesia is made in the same way, and the male is converted with it. But forasmuch as there is a certain affinity between the magnet and the iron, therefore our nature rejoices.) Take, then, the vapour which the Ancients commanded you to take, and cook the same with its own body until tin is produced. Wash away its blackness according to custom, and cleanse and roast at an equable fire until it be whitened. But every body is whitened with governed quicksilver, for Nature converts Nature. Take, therefore, Magnesia, Water of Alum, Water of Nitre, Water of the Sea, and Water of Iron; whiten with smoke.: Whatsoever ye desire to be whitened is whitened with this smoke, because it is itself white, and whitens all things. Mix, therefore, the said smoke with its faeces until it be coagulated and become excessively white. Roast this white copper till it germinates of itself, since the Magnesia when whitened does not suffer the spirits to escape, or the shadow of copper to appear, because Nature contains Nature. Take, therefore, all ye Sons of the Doctrine, the white sulphureous nature, whiten with salt and dew, or with the Flower of White Salt, until it become excessively white. And know ye, that the Flower of White Salt is Ether from Ethelia. The same must be boiled for seven days, till it shall become like gleaming marble, for when it has reached this condition it is a very great Arcanum, seeing that Sulphur is mixed with Sulphur, whence an excellent work is accomplished, by reason of the affinity between them, because natures rejoice in meeting their own natures. Take, therefore, Mardek and whiten the same with Gadenbe, that is, wine and vinegar, and Permanent Water. Roast and coagulate until the whole does not liquefy in a fire stronger than its own, namely, the former fire. Cover the mouth of the vessel securely, but let it be associated with its neighbour, that it may kindle the whiteness thereof, and beware lest the fire blaze up, for in this case it becomes red prematurely, and this will profit you nothing, because in the beginning of the ruling you require the white. Afterwards coagulate the same until you attain the red. Let your fire be gentle in the whitening, until coagulation take place. Know that when it is coagulated we call it the Soul, and it is more quickly converted from nature into nature. This, therefore, is sufficient for those who deal with the Art of Coins, because one thing makes it but many operate therein. For ye need not a number of things, but one thing only, which in each and every grade of your work is changed into another nature.

The Turba saith: Master, if you speak as the Wise have spoken, and that briefly, they will follow you who do not wish to be wholly shut in with darkness.

The Thirteenth Dictum.

Pythagoras saith:- We posit another government which is not from another root, but it differs in name. And know, all ye seekers after this Science and Wisdom, that whatsoever the envious may have enjoined in their books concerning the composition of natures which agree together, in savour there is only one, albeit to sight they are as diverse as possible. Know, also, that the thing which they have described in so many ways follows and attains its companion without fire, even as the magnet follows the iron, to which the said thing is not vainly compared, nor to a seed, nor to a matrix, for it is also like unto these. And this same thing, which follows its companion without fire, causes many colours to appear when embracing it, for this reason, that the said one thing enters into every regimen, and is found everywhere, being a stone, and also not a stone; common and precious; hidden and concealed, yet known by everyone; of one name and of many names, which is the Spume of the Moon. This stone, therefore, is not a stone, because it is more precious; without it Nature never operates anything; its name is one, yet we have called it by many names on account of the excellence of its nature.

The Turba answereth:- O! Master! wilt thou not mention some of those names for the guidance of seekers?

And he:- It is called White Ethelia, White Copper, and that which flies from the fire and alone whitens copper. Break up, therefore, the White Stone, and afterwards coagulate it with milk. Then pound the calx in the mortar, taking care that the humidity does not escape from the vessel; but coagulate it in the vessel until it shall become a cinder. Cook also with Spume of Luna and regulate. For ye shall find the stone broken, and already imbued with its own water. This, therefore, is the stone which we call by all names, which assimilates the work and drinks it, and is the stone out of which also all colours appear. Take, therefore, that same gum, which is from the scoriae, and mix with cinder of calx, which you have ruled, and with the faeces which you know, moistening with permanent water. Then look and see whether it has become a powder, but if not, roast in a fire stronger than the first fire, until it be pounded. Then imbue with permanent water, and the more the colours vary all the more suffer them to be heated. Know, moreover, that if you take white quicksilver, or the Spume of Luna, and do as ye are bidden, breaking up with a gentle fire, the same is coagulated, and becomes a stone. Out of this stone, therefore, when it is broken up, many colours will appear to you. But herein, if any ambiguity occur to you in our discourse, do as ye are bidden, ruling the same until a white and coruscating stone shall be produced, and so ye find your purpose.

The Fourteenth Dictum.

Acsubofen saith:- Master, thou hast spoken without envy, even as became thee, and for the same may God reward thee!

Pythagoras saith:- May God also deliver thee, Acsubofen, from envy!

Then he:- Ye must know, O Assembly of the Wise, that sulphurs are contained in sulphurs, and humidity in humidity.

The Turba answereth:- The envious, O Acsubofen, have uttered something like unto this! Tell us, therefore, what is this humidity?

And he:- Humidity is a venom, and when venom penetrates a body, it tinges it with an invariable colour, and in no wise permits the soul to be separated from the body, because it is equal thereto. Concerning this, the envious have said: When one flies and the other pursues, then one seizes upon the other, and afterwards they no longer flee, because Nature has laid hold of its equal, after the manner of an enemy, and they destroy one another. For this reason, out of the sulphureous mixed sulphur is produced a most precious colour, which varies not, nor flees from the fire, when the soul enters into the interior of the body and holds the body together and tinges it. I will repeat my words in Tyrian dye. Take the Animal which is called Kenckel, since all its water is a Tyrian colour, and rule the same with a gentle fire, as is customary, until it shall become earth, in which there will be a little colour. But if you wish to obtain the Tyrian tincture, take the humidity which that thing has ejected, and place it therewith gradually in a vessel, adding that tincture whereof the colour was disagreeable to you. Then cook with that same marine water until it shall become dry. Afterwards moisten with that humour, dry gradually, and cease not to imbue it, to cook, and to dry, until it be imbued with all its humour. Then leave it for several days in its own vessel, Until the most precious Tyrian colour shall come out from it to the surface. Observe how I describe the regimen to you! Prepare it with the urine of boys, with water of the sea, and with permanent clean water, so that it may be tinged, and decoct with a gentle fire, until the blackness altogether shall depart from it, and it be easily pounded. Decoct, therefore, in its own humour until it clothe itself with a red colour. But if ye wish to bring it to the Tyrian colour, imbue the same with continual water, and mix, as ye know to be sufficient, according to the rule of sight; mix the same with permanent water sufficiently, and decoct until rust absorb the water. Then wash with the water of the sea which thou hast prepared, which is water of desiccated calx; cook until it imbibe its own moisture; and do this day by day. I tell you that a colour will thence appear to you the like of which the Tyrians have never made. And if ye wish that it should be a still more exalted colour, place the gum in the permanent water, with which ye shall dye it alternately, and afterwards desiccate in the sun. Then restore to the aforesaid water and the black Tyrian colour is intensified. But know that ye do not tinge the purple colour except by cold. Take, therefore, water which is of the nature of cold, and steep wool therein until it extract the force of the

tincture from the water. Know also that the
Philosophers have called the force which proceeds
from that water the Flower. Seek, therefore, your
intent in the said water; therein place what is in
the vessel for days and nights, until it be clothed
with a most precious Tyrian colour.

The Fifteenth Dictum.

Frictes saith:- O all ye seekers after Wisdom, know that the foundation of this Art, on account of which many have perished, is one only. There is one thing which is stronger than all natures, and more sublime in the opinion of philosophers, whereas with fools it is more common than anything. But for us it is a thing which we reverence. Woe unto all ye fools! How ignorant are ye of this Art, for which ye would die if ye knew it! I swear to you that if kings were familiar with it, none of us would ever attain this thing. O how this nature changeth body into spirit! O how admirable is Nature, how she presides over all, and overcomes all!

Pythagoras saith:- Name this Nature, O Frictes!

And he:- It is a very sharp vinegar, which makes gold into sheer spirit, without which vinegar, neither whiteness, nor blackness, nor redness, nor rust can be made. And know ye that when it is mixed with the body, it is contained therein, and becomes one therewith; it turns the same into a spirit, and tinges with a spiritual and invariable tincture, which is indelible. Know, also, that if ye place the body over the fire without vinegar, it will be burnt and corrupted. And know, further, that the first humour is cold. Be careful, therefore, of the fire, which is inimical to cold. Accordingly, the Wise have said: "Rule gently until the sulphur becomes incombustible." The Wise men have already shewn to those who possess reason the disposition of this Art, and the best point of their Art, which they mentioned, is, that a little of this sulphur burns a strong body. Accordingly they venerate it and name it in the beginning of their book, and the son of Adam thus described it. For this vinegar burns the body, converts it into a cinder, and also whitens the body, which, if ye cook well and deprive of blackness, is changed into a stone, so that it becomes a coin of most intense whiteness. Cook, therefore, the stone until it be disintegrated, and then dissolve and temper with water of the sea. Know also, that the beginning of the whole work is the whitening, to which succeeds the redness, finally the perfection of the work; but after this, by means of vinegar, and by the will of Gcd, there follows a complete perfection, Now, I have shewn to you, O disciples of this Turba, the disposition of the one thing, which is more perfect, more precious, and more honourable, than all natures, and I swear to you by God that I have searched for a long time in books so that I might arrive at the knowledge of this one thing, while I prayed also to God that he would teach me what it is. My prayer was heard, He shewed me clean water, whereby I knew pure vinegar, and the more I did read books, the more was I illuminated.

The Sixteenth Dictum.

Socrates saith:- Know, O crowd of those that still remain of the Sons of the Doctrine, that no tincture can be produced without Lead, which possesses the required virtue. Have ye not seen how thrice-great Hermes infused the red into the body, and it was changed into an invariable colour? Know, therefore, that the first virtue is vinegar, and the second is the Lead of which the Wise have spoken, which if it be infused into all bodies, renders all unchangeable, and tinges them with an invariable colour. Take, therefore, Lead which is made out of the stone called Kuhul; let it be of the best quality, and let it be cooked till it becomes black. Then pound the same with Water of Nitre until it is thick like grease, and cook again in a very bright fire until the spissitude of the body is destroyed, the water being rejected. Kindle, therefore, above it until the stone becomes clean, abounding in precious metal, and exceedingly white. Pound it afterwards with dew and the sun, and with sea and rain water for 31 days, for 10 days with salt water, and 10 days with fresh water, when ye shall find the same like to a metallic stone. Cook the same once more with water of nitre until it become tin by liquefaction. Again cook until it be deprived of moisture, and become dry. But know that when it becomes dry it drinks up what remains of its humour swiftly, because it is burnt lead. Take care, however, lest it be burnt. Thus we call it incombustible sulphur. Pound the same with the sharpest vinegar, and cook till it becomes thick, taking care lest the vinegar be changed into smoke and perish; continue this coction for 150 days. Now, therefore, I have demonstrated the disposition of the white lead, all which afterwards follows being no more than women's work and child's play. Know, also, that the arcanum of the work of gold proceeds out of the male and the female, but I have shewn you the male in the lead, while, in like manner, I have discovered for you the female in orpiment. Mix, therefore, the orpiment with the lead, for the female rejoices in receiving the strength of the male, because she is assisted by the male. But the male receives a tingeing spirit from the female. Mix them, therefore, together, place in a glass vessel, and pound with Ethelia and very sharp vinegar; cook for seven days, taking care lest the arcanum smoke away, and leave throughout the night. But if ye wish it to put on mud (colour), seeing that it is already dry, again imbue with vinegar. Now, therefore, I have notified to you the power of orpiment, which is the woman by whom is accomplished the most great arcanum. Do not shew these unto the evil, for they will laugh. It is the Ethelia of vinegar which is placed in the preparation, by which things God perfects the work, whereby also spirits take possession of bodies, and they become spiritual.

The Seventeenth Dictum.

Zimon saith:- O Turba of Philosophers and disciples, now hast thou spoken about making into white, but it yet remains to treat concerning the reddening! Know, all ye seekers after this Art, that unless ye whiten, ye cannot make red, because the two natures are nothing other than red and white. Whiten, therefore, the red, and redden the white! Know, also, that the year is divided into four seasons; the first season is of a frigid complexion, and this is Winter; the second is of the complexion of air, and this is Spring; then follows the third, which is summer, and is of the complexion of fire; lastly, there is the fourth, wherein fruits are matured, which is Autumn. In this manner, therefore, ye are to rule your natures, namely, to dissolve ill winter, to cook in spring, to coagulate in summer, and to gather and tinge the fruit in autumn. Having, therefore, given this example, rule the tingeing natures, but if ye err, blame no one save yourselves.

The Turba answereth:- Thou hast treated the matter extremely well; add, therefore, another teaching of this kind for the sake of posterity.

And he:- I will speak of making lead red. Take the copper which the Master ordered you to take at the beginning of his book, combine lead therewith, and cook it until it becomes thick; congeal also and desiccate until it becomes red. Here certainly is the Red Lead of which the wise spake; copper and lead become a precious stone; mix them equally, let gold be roasted with them, for this, if ye rule well, becomes a tingeing spirit in spirits. So when the male and the female are conjoined there is not produced a volatile wife, but a spiritual composite. From the composite turned into a red spirit is produced the beginning of the world. Behold this is the lead which we have called Red Lead, which is of our work, and without which nothing is effected!

The Eighteenth Dictum.

Mundus saith to the Turba:- The seekers after this Art must know that the Philosophers in their books have described gum in many ways, but it is none other than permanent water, out of which our precious stone is generated. O how many are the seekers after this gum, and how few there are who find it! Know that this gum is not ameliorated except by gold alone. For there be very many who investigate these applications, and they find certain things, yet they cannot sustain the labours because they are diminished. But the applications which are made out of the gum and out of the honourable stone, which has already held the tincture, they sustain the labours, and are never diminished. Understand, therefore, my words, for I will explain unto you the applications of this gum, and the arcanum existing therein. Know ye that our gum is stronger than gold, and all those who know it do hold it more honourable than gold, yet gold we also honour, for without it the gum cannot be improved. Our gum, therefore, is for Philosophers more precious and more sublime than pearls, because out of gum with a little gold we buy much. Consequently, the Philosophers, when committing these things to writing that the same might not perish, have not set forth in their books the manifest disposition, lest every one should become acquainted therewith, and having become familiar to fools, the same would not sell it at a small price. Take, therefore, one part of the most intense white gum; one part of the urine of a white calf; one part of the gall of a fish; and one part of

46

the body of gum, without which it cannot be improved; mix these portions and cook for forty days. When these things have been done, congeal by the heat of the sun till they are dried. Then cook the same, mixed with milk of ferment, until the milk fail; afterwards extract it, and until it become dry evaporate the moisture by heat. Then mix it with milk of the fig, and cook it till that moisture be dried up in the composite, which afterwards mix with milk of the root of grass, and again cook until it be dry. Then moisten it with rainwater, then sprinkle with water of dew, and cook until it be dried. Also imbue with permanent water, and desiccate until it become of the most intense dryness. Having done these things: mix the same with the gum which is equipped with all manner of colours, and cook strongly until the whole force of the water perish; and the entire body be deprived of its humidity, while ye imbue the same by cooking, until the dryness thereof be kindled. Then dismiss for forty days. Let it remain in that trituration or decocting until the spirit penetrate the body. For by this regimen the spirit is made corporeal, and the body is changed into a spirit. Observe the vessel, therefore, lest the composition fly and pass off in fumes. These things being accomplished, open the vessel, and ye will find that which ye purposed. This, therefore, is the arcanum of gum, which the Philosophers have concealed in their books.

The Nineteenth Dictum.

Dardaris saith:- It is common knowledge that the Masters before us have described Permanent Water. Now, it behoves one who is introduced to this Art to attempt nothing till he is familiar with the power of this Permanent Water, and in commixture, contrition, and the whole regimen, it behoves us to use invariably this famous Permanent Water. He, therefore, who does not understand Permanent Water, and its indispensable regimen, may not enter into this Art, because nothing is effected without the Permanent Water. The force thereof is a spiritual blood, whence the Philosophers have called it Permanent Water, for, having pounded it with the body, as the Masters before me have explained to you, by the will of God it turns that body into spirit. For these, being mixed together and reduced to one, transform each other; the body incorporates the spirit, and the spirit incorporates the body into tinged spirit, like blood. And know ye, that whatsoever hath spirit the same hath blood also as well. Remember, therefore, this arcanum!

The Twentieth Dictum.

Belus saith:- O disciples, ye have discoursed excellently!

Pythagoras answers:- Seeing that they are philosophers, O Belus, why hast thou called them disciples?

He answereth:- It is in honour of their Master, lest I should make them equal with him.

Then Pythagoras saith:- Those who, in conjunction with us, have composed this book which is called the Turba, ought not to be termed disciples.

Then he:- Master, they have frequently described Permanent Water, and the making of the White and the Red in many ways, albeit under many names; but in the modes after which they have conjoined weights, compositions, and regimens, they agree with the hidden truth. Behold, what is said concerning this despised thing! A report has gone abroad that the Hidden Glory of the Philosophers is a stone and not a stone, and that it is called by many names, lest the foolish should recognise it, Certain wise men have designated it after one fashion, namely, according to the place where it is generated; others have adopted another, founded upon its colour, some of whom have termed it the Green Stone; by other some it is called the Stone of the most intense Spirit of Brass, not to be mixed with bodies; by yet others its description has been further varied, because it is sold for coins by lapidaries who are called saven; some have named it Spume of Luna;

some have distinguished it astronomically or arithmetically; it has already received a thousand titles, of which the best is: "That which is produced out of metals." So also others have called it the Heart of the Sun, and yet others have declared it to be that which is brought forth out of quicksilver with the milk of volatile things.

The Twenty-first Dictum.

Pandolfus saith:- O Belus, thou hast said so much concerning the despised stone that thou hast left nothing to be added by thy brethren! Howsoever, I teach posterity that this despised stone is a permanent water, and know, all ye seekers after Wisdom, that permanent water is water of mundane life, because, verily, Philosophers have stated that Nature rejoices in Nature, Nature contains Nature, and Nature overcomes Nature. The Philosophers have constituted this short dictum the principle of the work for reasonable persons. And know ye that no body is more precious or purer than the Sun, and that no tingeing venom: is generated without the Sun and its shadow. He, therefore, who attempts to make the venom of the Philosophers without these, already errs, and has fallen into that pit wherein his sadness remains. But he who has tinged the venom of the wise out of the Sun and its shadow has arrived at the highest Arcanum. Know also that our coin when it becomes red, is called gold; he, therefore, who knows the hidden Cambar of the Philosophers, to him is the Arcanum already revealed.

The Turba answereth:- Thou hast even now intelligibly described this stone, yet thou hast not narrated its regimen nor its composition. Return, therefore, to the description.

He saith:- I direct you to take an occult and honourable arcanum, which is White Magnesia, and the same is mixed and pounded with wine, but take care not to make use of this except it be pure and clean; finally place it in its vessel, and pray God that He may grant you the sight of this very great stone. Then cook gradually, and, extracting, see if it has become a black stone, in which case ye have ruled excellently well. But rule it thus for the white, which is a great arcanum, until it becomes Kuhul, closed up with blackness, which blackness see that it does not remain longer than forty days. Pound the same, therefore, with its confections, which are the said flower of copper, gold of the Indies whose root is one, and a certain extract of an unguent, that is, of a crocus, that is, fixed exalted alum; cook the four, therefore, permanently for 40 or 42 days. After these days God will show you the principle(or beginning) of this stone, which is the stone Atitos, of which favoured sight of God there are many accounts. Cook strongly, and imbue with the gum that remains. And know ye that so often as ye imbue the cinder, so often must it be desiccated and again humectated, until its colour turns into that which ye desire. Now, therefore, will I complete that which I have begun, if God will look kindly on us. Know also that the perfection of the work of this precious stone is to rule it with the residue of the third part of the medicine, and to preserve the two other parts for imbuing and cooking alternately till the required colour appears. Let the fire be more intense than the former; let the matter be cerated, and when it is desiccated it coheres. Cook, therefore, the wax until it imbibes the gluten of gold, which being desiccated, imbue the rest of the work seven times until the other two thirds be finished, and true earth imbibe them all. Finally, place the same on a hot fire until the earth extract its flower and be satisfactory. Blessed are ye if ye understand! But, if not, I will repeat to you the perfection of the work. Take the clean white, which is a most great arcanum, wherein is the true tincture; imbue sand therewith, which sand is made out of the stone seven times imbued, until it drink up the whole, and close the mouth of the vessel effectually, as you have often been told. For that which ye seek of it by the favour of God, will appear to you, which is the stone of Tyrian colour. Now, therefore, I have fulfilled the truth, so do I conjure you by God and your sure Master, that you show not this great arcanum, and beware of the wicked!

The Twenty-Second Dictum.

Theophilus saith: Thou hast spoken intelligently and elegantly, and art held free from envy.

Saith the Turba:- Let your discretion, therefore, explain to us what the instructing Pandolfus has stated, and be not envious.

Then he:- O all ye seekers after this science, the arcanum of gold and the art of the coin is a dark vestment, and no one knows what the Philosophers have narrated in their books without frequent reading, experiments, and questionings of the Wise. For that which they have concealed is more sublime and obscure than it is possible to make known in words, and albeit some have dealt with it intelligibly and well, certain others have treated it obscurely; thus some are more lucid than others.

The Turba answereth: Thou hast truly spoken.

And he:- I announce to posterity that between boritis and copper there is an affinity, because the boritis of the Wise liquefies; the copper, and it changes as a fluxible water. Divide, therefore, the venom into two equal parts, with one of which liquefy the copper, but preserve the other to Pound and imbue the same, until it is drawn out into plates; cook again with the former part of the venom, cook two to seven in two; cook to seven in its own water for 42 days; finally, open the vessel, and ye shall find copper turned into quicksilver; wash the same by cooking until it be deprived of its blackness, and become as copper without a shadow. Lastly, cook it continuously until it be congealed. For when it is congealed it becomes a very great arcanum. Accordingly, the Philosophers have called this stone Boritis; cook, therefore, that coagulated stone until it becomes a matter like mucra. Then imbue it with the Permanent water which I directed you to reserve, that is to say, with the other portion, and cook it many times until its colours manifest. This, therefore, is the very great putrefaction which extracts (or contains in itself) the very great arcanum.

Saith the Turba:- Return to thine exposition, O Theophilus!

And he:- It is to be known that the same affinity which exists between the magnet and iron, also exists assuredly between copper and permanent water. If, therefore, ye rule copper and permanent water as I have directed, there will thence result the very great arcanum in the following fashion. Take white Magnesia and quicksilver, mix with the male, and pound strongly by cooking, not with the hands, until the water become thin. But dividing this water into two parts, in the one part of the water cook it for eleven, otherwise, forty days, until there be a white flower, as the flower of salt in its splendour and coruscation: but strongly close the mouth of the vessel, and cook for forty days, when ye will find it water whiter than milk; deprive it of all blackness by cooking; continue the cooking until its whole nature be disintegrated, until the defilement perish, until it be found clean, and is wholly broken up (or becomes wholly clean). But if ye wish that the whole arcanum, which I have given you, be accomplished, wash the same with water, that is to say, the other part which I counselled you to preserve, until there appear a crocus, and leave in its own vessel. For the Iksir pounds (or contains) itself; imbue also with the residue of the water, until by decoction and by water it be pounded and become like a syrup of pomegranates; imbue it, therefore, and cook, until the weight of the humidity shall fail, and the colour which the Philosophers have magnified shall truly appear.

The Twenty-third Dictum.

Cerus saith:- Understand, all ye Sons of the Doctrine, that which Theophilus hath told you, namely, that there exists an affinity between the magnet and the iron, by the alliance of composite existing between the magnet and the iron, while the copper is fitly ruled for one hundred days: what statement can be more useful to you than that there is no affinity between tin and quicksilver!

The Turba answereth:- Thou hast ill spoken, having disparaged the true disposition.

And he:- I testify that I say nothing but what is true why are you incensed against me Fear the Lord, all ye Turba, that you Master may believe you!

The Turba answereth:- Say what you will.

And he:- I direct you to take quicksilver, in which is the male potency or strength; cook the same with its body until it becomes a fluxible water; cook the masculine together with the vapour, until each shall be coagulated and become a stone. Then take the water which you had divided into two parts, of which one is for liquefying and cooking the body, but the second is for cleansing that which is already burnt, and its companion, which [two] are made one. Imbue the stone seven times, and cleanse, until it be disintegrated, and its body be purged from all defilement, and become earth. Know also that in the time of forty-two days the whole is changed into earth; by cooking, therefore, liquefy the same until it become as true water, which is quicksilver. Then wash with water of nitre until it become as a liquefied coin. Then cook until it be congealed and become like to tin, when it is a most great arcanum; that is to say, the stone which is out of two things. Rule the same by cooking and pounding, until it becomes a most excellent crocus. Know also that unto water desiccated with its companion we have given the name of crocus. Cook it, therefore, and imbue with the residual water reserved by you until you attain your purpose.

The Twenty-fourth Dictum.

Bocascus saith:- Thou hast spoken well, O Belus, and therefore I follow thy steps!

He answereth:- As it may please you, but do not become envious, for that is not the part of the Wise.

And Bocascus:- Thou speakest the truth, and thus, therefore, I direct the Sons of the Doctrine. Take lead, and, as the Philosophers have ordained, imbue, liquefy, and afterwards congeal, until a stone is produced; then rule the stone with gluten of gold and syrup of pomegranates until it be broken up. But you have already divided the water into two parts, with one of which you have liquefied the lead, and it has become as water; cook, therefore, the same until it be dried and have become earth; then pound with the water reserved until it acquire a red colour, as you have been frequently ordered.

The Turba answereth:- Thou hast done nothing but pile up ambiguous words. Return, therefore, to the subject.

And he:- Ye who wish to coagulate quicksilver, must mix it with its equal. Afterwards cook it diligently until both become permanent water, and, again, cook this water until it be coagulated. But let this be desiccated with its own equal vapour, because ye have found the whole quicksilver to be coagulated by itself. If ye understand, and place in your vessel what is necessary, cook it until it be coagulated, and then pound until it becomes a crocus like to the colour of gold.

The Twenty-fifth Dictum.

Menabdus saith:- May God reward thee for the regimen, since thou speakest the truth! For thou hast illuminated thy words.

And they:- It is said because thou praisest him for his sayings, do not be inferior to him.

And he:- I know that I can utter nothing but that which he hath uttered; however, I counsel posterity to make bodies not bodies, but these incorporeal things bodies. For by this regimen the composite is prepared, and the hidden part of its nature is extracted. With these bodies accordingly join quicksilver and the body of Magnesia, the woman also with the man, and by means of this there is extracted our secret Ethelia, through which bodies are coloured; assuredly, if I understand this regimen, bodies become not bodies, and incorporeal things become bodies. If ye diligently pound the things in the fire and digest (or join to) the Ethelias, they become clean and fixed things. And know ye that quicksilver is a fire burning the bodies, mortifying and breaking up, with one regimen, and the more it is mixed and pounded with the body, the more the body is disintegrated, while the quicksilver is attenuated and becomes living. For when ye shall diligently pound fiery quicksilver and cook it as required, ye will possess Ethel, a fixed nature and colour, subject to every tincture, which also overcomes, breaks, and constrains the fire. For this reason it does not colour things unless it be coloured, and being coloured it colours. And know that no body can tinge itself unless its spirit be extracted from the secret belly thereof, when it becomes a body and soul without the spirit, which is a spiritual tincture, out of which colours have manifested, seeing that a dense thing does not tinge a tenuous, but a tenuous nature colours that which enters into a body. When, however, ye have ruled the body of copper, and have extracted from it a most tenuous (subject), then the latter is changed into a tincture by which it is coloured. Hence has the wise man said, that copper does not tinge unless first it be tinged. And know that those four bodies which you are directed to rule are this copper, and that the tinctures which I have signified unto you are the condensed and the humid, but the condensed is a conjoined vapour, and the humid is the water of sulphur, for sulphurs are contained by sulphurs, and rightly by these things Nature rejoices in Nature, and overcomes, and constrains.

www.ingramcontent.com/pod-product-compliance
Lightning Source LLC
Chambersburg PA
CBHW071750090426
42738CB00011B/2628